SINK

SINK

poems by

Desireé Dallagiacomo

—

Published by Button Poetry / Exploding Pinecone Press
Minneapolis, MN 55403 | http://www.buttonpoetry.com

—

Cover design: Nikki Clark

ISBN 978-1-943735-49-5

Contents

I was a late bloomer.
But anyone who blooms at all, ever, is very lucky.

—Sharon Olds

SINK

My First Altar

*Altar (noun): a place on which sacrifices are offered in worship,
or something sacrificed at the cost of something else.*

My first altar was my father's hands—no.

My first altar was my mother's body, a secret hideout in a woman's skin.

My first altar was my sister's fingers, folding tresses of hair until they were braids down my neck.

My first altar was a place with no name but a slow pulse I followed into brightness.

My first altar was a soft forgiveness.

My first altar was a story I made for myself. Where I call myself girl from many. I call myself daughter of the hunt, here only because a woman before me survived. A woman was never unmade and so she grew me.

My first altar was my body and then that of a starlit boy.

My first altar was the red bloom in my underwear, hid from the laundry and so it stayed a plume—evidence of growing.

My first altar was a cordless phone, whispered into under the covers late on a school night.

My first altar was a blood drawn by my hands. A thin line I dug myself.

My first altar was indeed a bloody song. A relentless ache to become.

My first altar was consensual on a grassy hill, white dress and walked up on by the school security guard.

My first altar was a cheap vibrator and an empty apartment. A body unwrapping under my hands.

My first altar was the night sky—wide and mine and still it belonged to no one at all.

My first altar was the dust kicked by my father's pickup truck before he became the myth I tell myself.

My first altar was when I undid the song they gave me, sang it backwards to myself. A girlbody before it was object. When I could throw a tantrum my body strung out with full arms and unslouched.

My first altar was a memory before the dark one, before darkness was my first language.

My first altar was a fat bitch looking in the mirror buttass naked.

My first altar was a chubby cunt served to a love like a meal and the one that knew what to do with it.

My first altar was my love's ass on a Sunday morning; nowhere to go and no need to cover up so we let the light in.

My first altar was made from red dirt, desert hands, a famine I have never seen but I know: the chorus of *never enough but it will do*. It was made when I was not yet, but just a wish for something more. Lineage is a wild animal that tames us and tethers us. Pulses us into being, pulls us from the ego of ourselves.

Can you believe that you, too, are someone's altar? You are someone's biggest dream, you, medicine baby, you, sprouted from an altar of ancestors into this great existence. And here you are, here you stand, here you stand. Pulsing.

When giving birth

it is possible to break

the strongest bone

in the body. Let the body

convince me

I can grow and shatter

at the same time.

For My Mother

Who spent whole life

      times with nothing but her girl

hood. Who pissed

      in a can in the attic

of her mother's house as a small

      burden.

And I know that I am half

      her or maybe more.

I'll tell you of the time

      she dug me out of the worst

grave in the cemetery

of my life. I'll tell you of the time

      she was so high, she forgot

I was living. And I will tell you that I love her

      still, still, and again.

Reno, Nevada

My grandfather broke
my father's arm
with a baseball bat.
After that, Dad was off
to Reno to learn
how to hang drywall.
There he lived
above a bar
and an old man
taught him how to build
a house with sheetrock,
and by the time
he met my mother
he was always
covered in white powder.
Trying to call himself a man
that could build a home from dust.

Medford, Oregon

Pregnant, my mother worked
in the hospital laundry room
folding sheets and washing
towels for 8 months. She did
this in exchange for a place
to have her 5th child.
Each year I get older,
a quiet ceremony for the girl
that was born in a bed
because a woman woke
every morning, building me
inside of her, and found
me a home before I had a name.
I do not know what you believe
love to be, but in our house it is that.

Señor Frogs

When 7 of us lived in the Motel 6
my father would get drunk at Señor Frogs across the parking lot.
He would come home spent on bitter

and turn my mother into a rag doll.
The night that she piled us, quiet as baby geese, into the station wagon,
after he let the liquor slither

his fingers around her throat, a dishrag
wrung dry. That night we left while he was soaking
filthy in the tub. This is how I learned to love.

Fleeting; in a panic; a frenzy;
watching as the wicked unfolds.

Strength

When I say my mother is strong, what I mean is she did crank 17 years & still has all her teeth. Smiles & teaches god about resilience. What I mean is she met my father on a cocaine deal. Coffee table, fresh snow nose dipped in white & still, rocked my brother to sleep. She, high as a crow murder & he, nuzzled to her. What I mean is months later my father broke her arm & she stayed. Broke a closed window with her head & she stayed. I mean broke nose no fuss.

I mean he broke everything but her.

What I mean is she can tell how much pressure a neck can take before it snaps. I mean 5 kids, no sedatives. I mean she has dug her grave & filled it again, again, again. & this is how we want our women: devour herself & we applaud. Say be open as coffin, except keep the dead in. What I mean is she is where strength goes to enjoy a view.

I mean each child hollowed from her a small death, I am the soul pulled from her, let me be her other life. Let me say fuck or forget strength, fuck or forget staying for sake of saving face, let me leave all that does not carry me.

Let me come from that & never be that.

Single Mothers Can Yell Wherever They Want

Nicole gets to get in trouble in private and I have
to do it in the apartment complex parking lot
and I guess that's what you get when your dad

is a doctor. You get to get yelled at with the door closed,
but my dad is a truancy. My mother screams

at me wherever she pleases. I guess that is her right—
when you are the edge of emptiness, you get to scream

at whatever you want if that makes you feel alive inside.
I'll take my licks in public, after all—every other kid

in the complex is dadless, too. We all share
the same missing limb, so we forget it's gone.

B on Elm Street Behind the Fairgrounds, 1999

Your father used to beat you with a vacuum tube and some people think that's not my story to tell but I tell it anyway. 4th grade recess. Long sweater and denim to your ankles. I ask what happened and you answer with the quiet leak of the lisp you still have. Then we play tetherball and never say another word of it. Draw curse words on the outside paneling of the trailer while your parents sleep through the weekend.

We don't have palatable memories of our fathers so we retell the ones we have like jokes so the other kids laugh instead of ask questions.

We are the seeds of the monsters poverty makes of men. We are not yet big enough to carry sorrow's weight slung on our backs. We are the children ducking the fists of our fathers, avoiding the punch line.

We learn to turn our ache into a good story. The insults our classmates bludgeon us with cannot steal the sweet sting of our laughter.

Our fathers' fists: one-liners we still know by heart.

Broken Sonnet for the Closeness of Grooming

The school nurse calls us in & picks through our
hair—an interrogation we'll turn up guilty
for. Tapes the lice to an index card &
sends us home. Sister slicks the mayonnaise

on my head, empties the whole jar—
this isn't our first rodeo. Her stern
hands cover each tress, blonde egg salad wrapped
in a Walmart bag. Each sister gets dressed

the same way & I understand shame
& I understand its relentless tug
toward intimacy despite our resistance.

I am supposed to be learning my times
tables but I am home with my sisters,
learning to lean in to each other,
no matter the mess.

10 Candles

But that's not the thing I want, I told her. It wasn't
that I only turn 10 once & it wasn't

that all my friends have dads & *why couldn't I
just have one*—not even on my birthday
do I get a dad. I think;

after all, I was turning 10 & my dad was smoking smack in an alley,
his eyes curdled into his skull, & I was blowing

out candles on a cake made to look like a giant bunny. Mom made me
a giant bunny and my dad got high & of course all I can think
is where is he.

No, it's not that, I tell her; the room was smoke
& I couldn't even think

of what to wish for in the long inhales
so I wish for a miracle—like for him to lose
his wallet or remember he left

his hat here or for him to miss
the bus and beg Mom to sleep on the couch
& maybe

she would say yes & let him into the party.
I blow into the air & tell Mom I wished for her

sunflowers to bloom but I really wish for his face
to appear, stumble through the smoke

& say   *surprise!*

Aunt Diana Opens the Trunk of Her Pathfinder and She Cannot Stop Crying as All the Presents for the Homeless Kids Fall Out

and I don't know why she jumped in the river or maybe she fell—
it's really not clear to me, but this story feels important.
I know that she's had more miscarriages than three and I do not hope

to understand that ache other than at a distance
and through my mother's mouth. Before they found her body,
she lost her mind and that's not too good of a choice

for dinner table conversation and if I'm being really honest
with you—I, too, know the begging ledge on the high bluff
of my heart whispering for me to leave the simple pain

of having a body at all.

The Gutter

When gutting the catfish, Mike would slit it straight down the belly.
Use his thumbs to pop out the eyes the way *fuck you* pops
from a broken boy's mouth. Mike was a surgeon. Precision.
Patience. A quiet thief. Mom would say, *Ya know,*
I don't know why you eat that shit. Catfish are the garbage disposals
of that goddamn river. They eat the shit the other fish won't touch.
We'd laugh and laugh the way we would. Pull pennies. Cigarette
butts. Marbles from the catfish belly.

Before Mike went to the penitentiary he was a small catfish—filling
with the shit the neighbors would not touch. Mike can pull
anything from the gutter, put it right back in it, too. He can cut
any beast in half. Prison slit him straight down the belly.
Pulled all that shit outta him. Laid it out on the table.
Now he's the biggest catfish I've ever seen.

Girlhood (noun)

: The state or time of being a bright bloom
: A plume of red circling the drain

: 1st cello, 3rd chair. Say nothing
: A slow roll down a wet hill

: A boy must call you *beautiful*

: A hymn each boy tries and tries to memorize and still fumbles

: Coroner
: Mortician

: That feeling you get when you are at the bottom
of the deep end and all out of breath

: To learn to clean up after your brother
: To learn to lie about your brother
: To learn to apologize for your brother
: To learn your brother when he will never learn you

: A hole dug and filled and dug and filled and dug and filled
and filled and filled and filled and filled and so on

With Vigor

The summer the AC breaks we sit in the backyard all day
& Mom runs the hose water over her painted toes & her belly is a soft
round home & it is out and her book is slouched on top.

I look in the mirror & hope someday clothes will fit me & all this fat
will stop spilling over everything. I look remarkably
like all the women I love.
And how did I learn to hate it so fiercely?

Pine Street, Taser

Sandy is Dad's new
girlfriend. A thin, brittle woman
who needed a place to sleep and slam crank
and so she found a sad man. He forgets about us
and they get a puppy and a one bedroom.
We live on Pine Street with Mom
and her new boyfriend (who will later
wail in the parking lot on 19th cradling
a knife and howling her name).
On weekends Sophie and I sit
in the shower and pretend
it is a tub. Throw the rag at each
other like confetti. Mom plucks
her eyebrows or pees and makes
certain we aren't touching
the moldy grout in the drain.
Okay, girls, 5 more minutes.

Once, while Mom is gone,
Sandy comes over unannounced
to show us the taser she found.

Next is the bright memory
that lets me forget what it means
to be left by a mother, a father,
and kept by a sister.

We try to be polite
and get Sandy to leave
on her own, but after
she burns a hole in the carpet
with her foreign treasure, laughing
through the thin stream of smoke,

Laura has had enough and so she cranks
up the heat as far as the dial will go.
Sandy starts sweating, *is it hot in here to you girls?*
with all of us lined on the couch
waiting for our cue—Laura eyes us hard
and shakes her head, a slow and certain command,
and so we all say *no*, sweat
dripping down our necks.
Sandy grabs her taser
and sits on the porch
to *smoke and cool off.*

Laura tucks us away,
locks the door,
shuts the blinds.
Presses her finger to her lips,
says, *Shhh.*

The Small, Breakable Nature of Gods

At what age do we ask children to imagine heaven
and who is there if not their missing

fathers? I've spent eons diving into his darkness—nothing.
I touch brown ground and think of the summer he made us

sleep in the bed of his truck lined with stolen carpet squares.
I gorge myself on this memory—my father's shoulders

in the parking lot of Tom's hotel where he lived and ran
an AA meeting for a while. I cannot remember his laugh

though I thought I would by now. His face fades and folds
into each year. I do not know any of his scars

and these things matter to me. I know my mother's body
as if I lived there. Each freckle and wrinkle and the day

they came. I feel the stitches on her shoulder from the Rottweiler
up the block. This is the godly nature of mothers. My mother

asks me about my favorite childhood memory, reaching
for something to redeem us from the long shadow of absence;

all I can replay is what was not there. Think
of all the things I'd write if I could erase the hum

of missing. I do not know what children with fathers
dream about, what they long for if not for someone

with their same face to tuck them in at night.
What do they think of with all that time on their hands?

Child Protective Services Takes B and All His Siblings on a Tuesday Afternoon

When we were kids, there was nothing

that took us from that glorious smallness but The State

came and changed that. Let me make this specific

trauma work for a poem: When I was sleeping,

The State took what was mine from me

and I have been running toward it ever since.

Knots

It is the 5th grade
and I've stopped
brushing my hair.
Laura fastens me
between her knees
and cuts the knots
that gather while
I sleep. She leaves
just enough hair
to cover the bald spots.

/ / /

And that's the trick,

really—girlhood

teaches us

that all it takes

is a small but beautiful

offering and no one

will notice you

are already halfway

gone.

/ / /

During class I reach into my frizzy halo and rub the empty
spots on my tiny skull, already so full of doubt without

you here. Your mother is in doing a 6-year bid
and your father is at home with his head heavy, well

into a dream without you in it. I think I can say
this will not be the last season in which I want to evaporate

from this speedtrap town—where we find ourselves on a map
by our proximity to all that is bigger than us.

It will be 10 years before we are old enough to not be children
of the state. And I will be mine and you will be in a home

you choose, I think. There will be a time when this heavy sadness
does not own me. I can imagine the loneliness

shaken from me by the blurry distance that years make—
but today you are not here. All that is here is this empty,
is this unending.

Origin Story

It was an accident, says my mother. My father,
not paying attention, swung the chainsaw
back too far too fast and Michael just *got in the way,*

chain caught his cheek and that's the end
of it. When they arrived home from the woods,
my mother says my father walked into the trailer

said, *We got a problem*
with the boy—that's what Dad called Mike,
the boy. Mike, 7 years old, walks in, face a canvas

of pale pinks and shucked reds.
All 3 layers of skin cut clean down to the bone
by the machine in our father's hands.

Your brother didn't make a sound, Mom says. *Never*
made a peep. Not even on the way
to the hospital. The surgeon did it for free,

Mom tells me years later.
We were poor as shit and he knew it. He said
if your father brought him 2 cords

of wood up to his cabin, he'd do it for free.
My father agreed, and just like my father,
never made good on the deal. *Just like your father,*

Mom tells me now, *to leave*
him hanging after he saved your brother's life.
On the playground Mike would peel back

the gauze, show all his friends the chainsaw
gash across his cheek,
now hardened & marked,

the cicatrix our father split himself.
28 years later and everyone still wants him

for his scars. The 5 on his stomach from a celly
in San Quentin—a toothbrush chiseled to a shiv.
The 6-inch gash on the back of his skull

—smashed into the pavement on 16th street.
His left eye pops out of his socket when he coughs
—the first time he was jumped in Tracy.

All 10 fingers
—each broken and healed twice.
Each mark has birthed him into a seamless clearing.

Each scar another felled tree.
And I think that's what a father is
—a blade that never stops cutting.

Everything to Call Him Before *Rapist*

The neighbor.
The boy up the block.
Grocery bagger at Food Maxx.
The gas station clerk at 7-11.
Father to a 3 year old. 6'2".
Grandfather's caretaker.

Friend.

The hum of the dryer.
A few dates and long walks to nowhere.
The room in the basement.
The laugh that took the tension.
The *oh c'mon* over, over, over

until it went dark.

Bought me lunch each Wednesday.
Opened doors.
Stiffened shoulders at other men,
kept them away like boys who like me do.
The split of a pelvis.
Sandpaper between legs.

Wishbone snap.

Ignored friend request (but never deleted).

Secret qualifier.

The shame after the shame.
The boy that is friends with all the cool girls.
The face that appears when I close my eyes.

The twice dirtied secret.
White toothy smile.
Months' worth of split open Venus razors.
Flinches at a new kiss.

BB bullet lodged into the tin can of me.

Apple corer.

Cherry pitter.

Coin tossed

in an empty well.

Be Mine

I worked my hands to the bone to sew shut
the mouth of each friend who called it *rape*.

At night, in the privacy of my head, your voice
was a single television always on in the background.
I tried to say it wasn't what it was.

Each dusk I'd kick through the gravel
to your house & my boyfriend never knew.

It was *our secret* and *after all,
we weren't doing anything wrong.*

Twirled in the chair & laughed
at all the jokes that I didn't get.

I carved my name into your desk.
Dotted the *i* with a heart.

When I wrote *be mine*
I didn't mean like this.

In State Prison, No One Keeps Their Underwires

We drive 4 and a half hours twice and we are getting through
the gates this time. The guard says, *no wires.* I say, *huh?*

He says, *take it off.* The guard makes me march
my bra out to the car and in the parking lot I unhinge.

I strip down and I don't even really want to see my brother
but my mother would cry on the phone again if he spent

another night cursing her out from the payphone. So I undo
for her. Sacrifice my skin for a woman that has nothing from men

except nostalgia. My shirt pressed to my nipples, Mom
and Mike not allowed to touch but catching up,
my arms crossed the whole visit.

Pleasant Valley State Prison with Inmate Number F-49837

Mike's been arrested enough times to call it a part-time job,
and he's still alive. Pulled over and beat by the pigs

in our neighborhood, Chapmantown, though everyone he cut
his teeth on is dead. Killed at a house party, while locked up, or shot

in a drive-by—and it's no coincidence—all while Mike
was away on a bid in Coalinga, High Desert, San Quentin,

shared a block with Charles Manson—*racist sonofabitch*,
Mike spits. Both held by the invisible cloak of whiteness,

a different density but the lynchpin still. Navigating this hard
truth is one of the great stumbles of my life. Maybe I'll learn

to say it better some day. Sometimes our kind of white boy breaks
from the shell of the Middle of Nowhere he became

himself in but most times he turns into the man who votes
a rapist over the free world. Carries a baseball bat laced

with nails to keep his little sister safe—violence is masculinity's
garter belt. All my uncles hold fast. Anyway, the boys

Mike did his longest bids with call him *Rednose*. The Screws
call him *Crazy White Boy* and most folks keep their distance.

But not me. Blood and memory tether me to the sad beast of him,
so I sit in the waiting room, wait my turn with all the other women

as we stare off, aglow under the fluorescence waiting for our man's
number to be called.

A Bluejay Flies into the Mental Hospital

and the girl that drank Drano stripped her throat just bigeye open-mouth grins and gasps and the boy that used a screwdriver to dig *kill me* into his forearm who buries his head behind the curtain is made to look by the jay and the girl I share a room with who tried to hang herself with a clear bra strap laughs until she falls into a coughing fit and the adults are so taken by this dashing something so splashed with brightness in our morning session they go bonkers hushing walkie talkies the whole 9 and something awakens in us and they hate when this happens when we all do not decide to feel we just f e e l and so in dives the jay blue as morphine into our made gray lives squawk, panic, try to fly away and I sit and still

I am. Everything

goes quiet and color splashes everywhere in this pit of a room.

(Hold on before I go any further think back: before this moment I am the girlghost and no matter the year or the place it's the same the social worker looks at me and even she flinches at my nothingness my invisible and I say I'm dying inside and she says I'm not that I'm *feeling anxious* I say I feel like a self floating above myself and she calls it *dissociation* I say I can feel my father chiseling his initials on the inside of my femur can't you hear it and she calls it *PTSD* I say I cannot unclench from the bedsheets in my memory she says *let go* I say I feel like the Grand Canyon moments before it became the Grand Canyon she tells me to *count backward from 10*

and she must not know I am the miraculous girl who swallowed 100 pills and did not die and the other girls know they halfway committed to killing themselves and they

think I am something else entirely because everyone knows
I should be dead.)

A boy who has never talked to any of us stands in the center of the
room outstretches his hand and the jay lands on his finger just like
that so we slow our breath and he walks to the window so high
above us all and he stands on his tiptoes on the table with his arm
all the way up and

out it goes.

Sink

I was my mother/her daughter when I learned to almost kill myself.
When I could no longer pretend the sadness/anguish was not swallowing
me. I kept 100 pills down long enough to be kissed by every eager EMT—
toads turning me to a real woman. Strapped to the stretcher, I wailed into
the hospital asylum. My wrists, cut red/carnations bloomed from soiled
body. Funeral skin trimmed with straight razor. Wilted altar for blood be-
fore me: Aunt Kelly: shotgun between teeth bathroom wall her brief con-
stellation. Great Grandma: rifle pushed pulled into the folds of her. Aunt
Diana: vodka/vicodin/SUV off the cliff/belly up in the river. Sister: razor-
blade bathtub. Grandma: vomit until she disappears. I open my mouth,
hope my mother's sad heart does not stumble drunk out of me. I am a
body/I am a scrapbook of survivor's guilt—turn each page, watch women
make ugly shrine of their/my bones. Fish out the demon by slitting its
throat— (when I say DEMON I do mean me). Maybe I wanted to float/
sink/be still long enough to see what my insides look like, what my heart
sounds like in slow motion. Each dragging gulp

of blood a glutton. Selfish heart, listen. I cannot tell this story about my-self. It has to be about someone that I love. My mother scratches at her skin so viciously she is a field of ripened sores. I recite it in dreams, boats that I know are my mother/me, sinking. I am dumping buckets of our blood from inside of her/me. And this is living—being so close to death you paint it on your skin. Why can't the women I look like open without a blade? Why can we only let coroners/surgeons see in us? Can I tell you I chased the pills with flattened Sprite, felt them swell in my throat? Blacked out, woke 8 days later, the whole room maroon. Sister Laura always comb-ing vomit from my hair, readying two braids to crawl down my selfish back. Or even that the mental hospital has windows thick as an iced-over lake. How we were salmon beneath, hungry for someone to drop a line, catch, release, briefly save us from this bloody birth stream, this lesson on inheritance. And aren't I that? I am the most unreliable narrator. I lie through my stitched wrists, my seam an invisible fishing line. Oh, how this love/lineage drops into me, begs me to hold my breath, and sink.

Grief Vignettes for Aunt Diana

My aunt Diana and I are both the family's babies. Both born blonde as dandelions. In the spring, we both plucked all of our petals from the stem. We are the same shell, different turtles tucked inside.

/ / /

It is spring here, and my mother over the telephone is the river that floats my aunt Diana into me through static. The shell of her is found drowned down river and no one is inside of it.

/ / /

There is a photo from 1969, a tiny blonde girl playing volleyball in the park. She used to say that if she didn't know better, she would say it was me.

/ / /

My aunt Diana gave me my first fishing pole. Taught me the river's want and ache. The way it taunts like a hungry mouth. Spring is the river's most starved season. Salivating from a frozen winter, its violent lips lick the cliff's edge.

/ / /

I have dreamt my body into parts—ripped this heart from its shell. How I cannot imagine her dead. How I see her in my mirror.

/ / /

A fisherman found her, pulled her out with his net. The coroner knew it was her only by her teeth.

/ / /

My mother's voice on the telephone is her baby sister's body floating down river. I cannot swim to her fast enough.

/ / /

I have no one to tell this story to. There is no language to say a body that could be confused for mine beckoned itself to the surface once all the life was wrung out of it.

/ / /

My mother says that when the police knocked, she knew what they were going to tell her.

/ / /

The body beckons itself back to its birth stream no matter how far it has strayed. I am a salmon in these hungry waters. One day, I will, too, die by the river. Born anew, dandelion, carried back into spring.

Written 5 Years after Your Body Was Found

Some say you got drunk and fell in the river
and the April or maybe May cold held you

down for a while. We used to camp at Cherry Lake,
Whiskeytown, Cohasset for a time or two, Mendocino.

The water there never took you for that spin
but this one was different.

The Sacramento River ran along the edge of town
and we'd fish there with line and a 2x4

sitting on the tree roots and you'd let me get in
the canoe with Uncle. Those are the sweetest days

that lick the wound of your memory

floating belly up south in the Umpqua.
I don't like to talk about it, but yes it's true—

you live in my dreams and I won't bore you
with the details, but there is water and breathing inside of them.

This is how our kind go to the great beyond. The unforgiving earth will
drag our kin into it and won't let go.

Ours have been the stewards of this land, raised young
with it and treated it well. I won't blame it for this.

I want to tell you that I called the sheriff,
my mother too spun dizzy with that good grief of you;

they didn't have much to say. Some say you went mad
in 2004, but I think you've always been and it won this time.

Leaving you undone in another body
of water. It was the month the salmon buck their way to death,

and I'll say I don't think you are the same
but you made it, sweet girl. To the end

of your own world and there you left us.
All evidence of you washed downstream.

Women like us, from a place cold and parentless, submit
to the grandest mother, and I imagine your last breath as a gift.

When I was a wordless baby we shared a room
in a government apartment in a town no one knows

and that makes you superimposed on me. There's more
to family than just blood. My want for you after yours has run

gone is all the proof I need. Do you live there, in the shallow home
of my bones, maybe? A part of me that never opens

the blinds but hears me wanting for you. There is no permanence
in our lineage except the blood of my mother's kin.

You would be 50 this year. Could it be that a life ends
when it should and you were never going to be 50?

I know your biggest haunt was your want to be a mother
and you should know that you were. To me. A mother

I was given by my mother. That's what a sister is: a tentacle
of the matriarch. I chase the memories of you like headlights

in the forest. I feel them slipping and I jot them down like a clue.
I don't believe in ghosts,

but I do believe in hunting out the haunting.
In secret, someone once told me your husband was forced to kill

his dog with a machete when he was a boy, and so his selfhood
was made from the knife. I don't want to reminisce and imagine

the myth of how the water took you from us but I do.
Once, when we were sleeping on a tarp in Cherry Hill

in the early summer of 1997, I woke in the black pitch of a forest
and walked into the night to pee in the woods

and what some people don't know is that when the quiet
is the only sound, the screech of the river makes things move

in a different rhythm. Before I knew it, I was ankle deep
in it and that memory I hold fast to. Was that you, too?

Did the darkness lead you to the river? My heart says
you jumped in, but my mother doesn't think so. It is against

our nature to believe the soil will turn on us when we treat
it like a sibling. I believe the river was your first and most true

love, so in my bones I say you did it to yourself. I do not blame you for
that. Once you're in over your head it's hard to turn back.

I remember the season you lived
in the Oregon winter, camped out by the river

with no home and no love but a sister's and that is the only home you
ever had. A kin's heart and a river's mouth is the land you

come from. And, truly, in the end you lived
there, gave your last and let the earth bury you

in a unmarked grave.

13 Ways of Looking at a Rapist

After Wallace Stevens

Your mother's boyfriend but not to you.

It's like you're coughing. It's in the middle of dinner
and everyone is staring and maybe someone acts like they notice
and then they ask you if you'll leave because it's too loud
and no one can do anything about it so you go
and cough until you can come back
and be fucking quiet about it already.

We are on the phone, his name in her voice.
She's crying and parked in the alley and she says
she was 14 and he choked her.

All my friends have them. You'd think we collect them
on purpose at this point.

Right swipe on Tinder and he never asked once.

Your teenage crush.

In the White House.

Once my boyfriend paid $240 to take me to laugh at his jokes.

Me too.

A slow simmer and before I even knew
the water was boiling he was done.

You honestly, truly did love him and still
you know it's true.

He was a good date before that.

You saw them holding hands and you knew that she loved him;
you once did, too. Even after he took your name and buried it
in the basement. How you hope she never finds it
clawing its way out from underneath them.

Thighs Say

My thighs say thunderous. My thighs say too fat for skinny jeans. Say
wide. Say open. My thighs say cellulite. Bad tattoo. Say stretch marks.
Pockmarks. Ingrown hair. My thighs feel upset that you only offered
one bite of your Ben & Jerry's Cherry Garcia. My thighs say more,
please. More room. More beat dropped. My thighs say we can dance
all night. My thighs want your thighs to work a little bit harder.
My thighs are always the elephant in the dressing room. My thighs
say what the fuck is a thigh gap? My thighs hate Urban Outfitters.
Hate Banana Republic. Hate American Apparel. Love the 1 pair
of jeans we wear 4 times a week because they're the only ones
that fit right.

My thighs hope your thighs have a great day. My thighs want you
to stop calling this body soft fruit. My thighs say feminism, bitch.
My thighs say we have always been the tattletale of the androgynous.
Cannot pull the feminine out of us. My thighs make a mockery
of shorts. Stay spilling over at the everything's seam.

My thighs say we don't want your praise, man
on the street corner. Man in the parking garage.
Man in Walgreens while we're buying tampons.

My thighs say we are every man's
wet dream, even when we beg
not to be. Even when we close
like locked jaw. When we ask

nicely. Beg him to stop. When we never asked for your eyes. Hands.
Mouth. My thighs remember bruise. Beckon. They know quake.
Know crave. My thighs have been shame. Fear. Still are most
days. My thighs know when to tighten. Stop all the space
taking up. My thighs know empty. All we do is doorway
for this body's ability to woman. We have always been

this. Axis of this balancing act of woman. Do we make you
uncomfortable? Is this too much praise, gospel of this body?
We don't know small. Our everything is too big. Monstrous.
Sturdy. Pillars for this woman body. Armor. We stay
the stilts that carry this heart. This everything woman.

My thighs say you don't know shit about envelope.
Coil through the quiver. Pull love into you like we
do. My thighs say leave the lights on. We spent
a lifetime hiding. Shake out of this shame.

We are the ruthless twins. Too strong to
not run toward everything light. My
thighs say don't tell us shit about
what we say about this body.
This heavy body. It is light.
It is light. It is ours.

We gatekeepers. Welcome
committee. My thighs say
come in to this when
we say. This is ours.
All of this. Ours.

Salties

In Australia, there are 2 types of crocodiles,
my friend Kaye tells me. *Salties & freshies.*
Salties used to be freshies until they developed filters
under their tongues for the saltwater. There are 2 Salties
near Kaye's house in Darwin and I am on the edge of my seat here,
waiting to hear about all the bodies they've claimed.
She says most locals just avoid them—nothing too dramatic.
They can sprint 100 meters at once, so naturally
folks just stay out of their way. I think of this
when I am on a plane from Auckland to Los Angeles,
and for some reason the beach is in my chest
and the water is my blood, but this is where
the metaphor stops making sense
because I'm the crocodile,
not my love or my mother
or the memory in place of my father.
And here I am, showing my teeth at anyone who comes too close.

It Took My Mother 3 Days to Give Birth to Me

and you wonder why I take so long to let things go.

Nine

It was the morning you smashed the coffee mug
my mother made me on the kitchen floor.

It was the night you told me to *stop acting
like a goddamned child* in front of your father.

It was the sunrise I woke and you were half-
dressed in the shower with the whiskey bottle shattered

into the drain. This was what I learned of love.
Love, love is to break open

all the things we thought we understood.

Joliet Street

I knew it wasn't going to work when you told me
to *just relax a little* with your face between my legs
like your MFA could mansplain me an orgasm.
But I kept fucking you

for 10 months after that. In your unkempt house, god awful
sheets and your cabinets always open like a dirty mouth.
Your inability to wash a dish and the piss crust
around your toilet seat. The crock-pot's maggot infestation.

With 6 months left until we expired,
you asked me to move into your shotgun
house, and there was where we really rotted.
Two years after we met,

we hated each other. One year after we met,
we hated each other but we did not know
we hated each other. We just kept ramming
our bodies like two goats on a bluff. I couldn't leave

our little hell, so I just looked away
every time you undressed and hoped it would be quick.

One Side of an Ongoing Dialogue with Sharon, My Therapist

My father dropped out of high school I was the high school I might be as crazy as my father Sharon sometimes when my grief is a mechanical bull like today I want to love anybody but me but nobody else wants to ride Sharon the poems are anthills inside of my brain they won't stop hiding inside of me that's why I wear my problems like they are from the discount bin at a garage sale Sharon people never really leave they just hide inside of me like my father my sister on the kitchen floor the man's knife in my brother's back in the alleyway the man's sign outside of the clinic that's why my words have to claw from behind my teeth Sharon why do we keep bringing up my father he is a chainsaw in the forest of my bones he is a barbed wire fence to my lover's bear hug Sharon why won't he leave why won't he come home my father was a bully he walked out like our family was detention while the boys put firecrackers in the mouth of my depression Sharon being this sad all the time is really hard

nobody wants to develop my negatives in their darkroom

sometimes my head is a wishing well and I fall inside and I'm a coin flipping like a child I don't know how to swim Sharon I swear to God Sharon I will break my own heart clean in half before anyone else even cracks it I want him to know that Sharon I want him to know that he is made of glue love is a terrifying beast Sharon I hate when people pretend something is what it is not you know when they pretend that watching me implode is love it's not love it's a spectacle I don't want to be a spectacle anymore Sharon people are always looking at me who cares that I'm half bald I know I am my ex boyfriend's girlfriend is bald she was when I met her while she was giving him a blowjob in the bathroom of our apartment you know I have a sister that I've never met my mom is not her mom she's the same age as my real sister Laura do you get it yet I know shitty right sometimes I can feel my heartbeat in my throat I swear my heart is trying to tell my mouth it can't find the right words maybe that's why I yell I say the wrong things I play chicken with myself I want to see who's gunna leave it's everybody mostly everybody leaves Sharon who doesn't leave when I was like 7 my mom left my brother went to prison when I was 14 I'm 28 Sharon he is still in prison he is still gone and now Sharon and now he gets mad at me when I don't write him letters he left why do I have to write him Sharon why can't I leave sometimes when I get really frustrated I hit the hallway wall and I pull my hair maybe that's why I cut it all off yes I know that anger is always a secondary emotion so then what's the first fear anxiety sadness loneliness aren't you supposed to tell me these things Sharon aren't you supposed to know Sharon it's weird I cry in doorways all the time it's so silly why am I standing in a doorway crying that's stupid I like being alone I just hate leaving

**I tell you *my heart*
*is like an avocado seed***

If left for too long
it'll burst right through my skin

The Funny Wind of the Heart Is Not a Reliable Weathervane

I do not know how long regret lived in our house
before it finally evicted us. It was so loud

I used to fix it a plate at dinner; our only child. Together
we were an empty silo, measuring silence by the gallon.

Our loneliness was our rowboat. I'd throw
a line out and wait for the dead to surface.

We were so hungry we would have eaten anything.
I would clench your memory in my mouth, a meal

I'd tear to pieces. My heart
was an estuary you could never survive inside.

Sorrow was our favorite place to undress, hoping time
would be a forgiving God. We'd pray his hands

would be soft the day we turned our bodies over to starve
the quiet animal of our indifference.

The Autumn I Found Out You Were Dead

I finally cleared the attic. I threw away
the blanket you used to clean up my vomit
the first night I accidentally told you I hated you.
The new person in my bed whispers
about the fountains in Germany, but all I can think
of is your knees in Mississippi the fourth time
we fell for each other. I kiss him and he becomes
a hot air balloon filled with you.
He tastes like a dream I want to shake out of.
I stopped looking at plane tickets to the forest
we used to promise to name our children after.
All the trees have fallen. I still hear them echo
your laugh. The day Max buried you,
I put your teeth in a jar under the floorboards.
My mother never stopped asking why
I let them stay. There are things that left
when the train pulled away from the station.
And there are things that stayed, like an epitaph
of everything we couldn't stomach to bury with the body.

Jemez Springs, New Mexico

My friend Jo Ann tells me
that the people
in Jemez Springs
are so unhappy
because the mountain
town is surrounded by mesas
creating darkness
for an unreasonable
amount of time.
I don't know if this is true,
but I know the pain
of darkness stacked
upon darkness
with a light just out of view.

I Break Like a Fever

For Sam, Lexi, Beck, Kaycee, Julia, and Sasha

I can't hear anyone talk about love without thinking
plane crash. Each face, a choir of heartache. Costumes of loss.
Trumpet voices in the second line marching band
out of my funeral home heart. What I know about grief
I learned in a winter in New Orleans. Nights I would drive
the city, end up by some massive body of water. Sob
at the shoreline. Stare the beast in its face, and it didn't give
a shit how loud I screamed. It roared back louder.
If there is anything that breaking like a wave has taught me
it is that when love leaves it doesn't always shut the door
on its way out. The last time I left my heart wide open,
the hurricane in me got so bad, my best friend
had to call me every single morning for 3 months straight
just to make sure I was still alive. Because sometimes
that is the hardest thing to do—just stay alive.
In this zombie heart planet. People walking around pretending
to exist. It looks so goddamned easy to play along, but listen
for the people with the upturned palms whispering,
Here, take my sweater. It's fucking freezing out there.
You compass. Waterfall smile. Umbrella chest. Grand Canyon elbows.

You deserve to make it home.

Ignore the radio static lost signal hearts when all you want
are directions back to the lighthouse where your own love lives
through this goddamned sea storm. Keep swimming.
That kind of love only stays when it has to
and it stays every single time.
My mother folded laundry in the hospital I was born in
so that I wouldn't first see the world as some back road
barn in Oregon. I come from a heart made from sturdy

hands. A heart made to set sail. Ride the waves. Keep swimming.
The storm is always thick. It is always loud.
The road home is small; it is quiet. It is a warm you have to get
used to. It is a ship made from everyone that ever told you
they loved you and stayed when your heart slammed shut
so loud you could not say it back. Sometimes I am so spilling over
with feelings, I have to lock myself in my bedroom, pull the blankets
up over my head, turn the lights off so I don't explode
out all of my insides. I am full. I am boiling over. I am fragile.
I am terrified to say that. To say I break like a fever.

I break like a bad habit.

Like a windshield.

Like a wave.

Sometimes love doesn't stay, but motherfuck, when it does
it is worth every person that ever told you that you were not enough.
That tried to put your love's honest flame out,
that confused your birthday candle kiss, firecracker mouth
for some blazing forest. For some torched chapel.
Let them run out of you like a house up in flames.
They won't be the first. They won't be the last.

Pull the fire alarm. Let it rain.

The Best Way I Can Tell You about the Resiliency of Tenderness Is with a Portrait of the Pitbull I Share My Bed With

Spent half his life on a chain in the Louisiana heat
and still hides behind my legs when the door slams.

Talk // Talk // Talk

He asks me why I talk so loud so so loud
loud loud he asks so loudly. He asks
me, *Why*. Why I *talk*. He asks, *Why talk
so loud?* So loud. Why so so so loud? I
talk, so he asks. I talk so loud but I am
not allowed to talk so loud. I talk and
       talk
           talk
               talk
                    and talk.
Talk? I ask. Loudly. *Why*, he asks. WHY,
he talks so loud. *Why*, he asks so loud.
Wide eyed, he asks. I ask
        — am I allowed?
He stalks me and asks why I am so loud.
I talk
      louder
        louder
          louder still
he asks about each thing we talk about.
Each thing I talk about, a thing he wants
to quiet.
A thing he wants.
        He wants,
           and wants,
              and can't
stay quiet. He's so so so loud, and he
      asks
        asks
          asks.
Each thing he thinks his thing. Each
thing he thinks, he asks. Says it so loud,
and he is always allowed to ask all the

things he thinks, but I am not allowed.
I cannot ask out loud. He asks me why I
talk, and each thing

        he plucks from my mouth
is his.

Where Did You Get that Pick-Up Line?
You Should Drop It Back Off

Excuse me, sir. Are you the moon? Because I need you
238,900 miles away from me.

You make me want to go to Hogwarts
so I can make you disappear.

Oh my god you're so funny . . . looking.

Are we at the rodeo?
Because this conversation is bullshit.

You look so strong. Why don't you go take down the patriarchy
and heteronormative ideals while I sit over here and watch?

Your advances and excessive touching and jokes are all so funny
I decided to tell them to my lawyer.

You make me think all kinds of naughty things,
like where to hide a body.

If I had a nickel for every time I heard that line,
I would throw them all at you.

You wanna know how I got these guns?
Working out because I'm terrified of violent masculinity!

You remind me of 1919,
the way I don't have a say in this exchange.

Can I have 78% of the time you're giving me, please?

You and my bra have something in common;
you are both annoying and make everything less enjoyable.

You must be a tree the way I see you and think,
leave.

Sum of Her Parts

5 and B's father calls me *bitch* when I refuse
to give my bike to the neighbor boys.

7 I'm *bitch* when I spit in Jacob's hair for stealing
my ice cream cone.

12 I'm suspended for punching Steven
in the face at the bus stop. Called me *bitch*,
and all the bite I watched my father strangle
out of my mother runs my fist into his face.

/ / /

As a girl, I was made to know that I come from a
brigade of bitches—women who will make you
eat your words with a quick snarl. Got rid of all
the men who would not say our proper names.
Learned that if you do not use your mouth, he
will use it against you, as throne to call himself
mighty—but what is a boy but a boy preparing to
be a bigger boy?

/ / /

14 when I refuse my boyfriend a blowjob on the bus.

18 when I tell the bouncer to keep his *fucking hands off of me.*

21 when I boo the comedian through his entire joke
about ripping his girlfriend to pieces from the inside
of her vagina.

23 I'm *bitch* when the man ogles me on the corner, licks
his lips, so I throw a rock through his back window.

/ / /

Women in my family do not worry about being named *bitch*;
we worry about being buried at the hands of the men we raise.

A Man Says to a Woman I Love, *If I Caught You in Bed with Someone Else, I'd Shoot You Both*

Alexis loves a man that I hate & so I imagine
12 hours' worth of ways to skin him. I feel the blade
on the inner edge of the butter knife & imagine
him on the other end of it & yes, I know
there are better knives to kill a man but this one will do just fine.
I imagine him hung ankles tied with a blowdryer. A corkscrew
slowly turned into each finger. My sister's kitchen shears
steadily sliding up his calf.

Men do not own violence. I have, in my life, held tight
to the bloodrush that a threat gives me. But that ownership
is too exhausting a task. Wishing a hex is survival
& it is not the same as enacting it but I don't
want that weight.

I have already used my temper & imagined him lost
at sea in a cork rowboat with nothing but his goddamn hands.
Imagined his dick covered in maggots. His throat full of rotten olives.
He says, *Without you, I may as well kill myself,*
& this is the kind of abuse meant for women
trained in the staying, trained in the get through,
trained in the no matter what of love & so instead
of wishing him dead, I wish Alexis love. I wish her
a life full of loves so big she forgets this small man,
this ignorant & insignificant piece of shit.
I wish her an orgasm every hour on the hour
the day she forgets his name. I wish her a husband
so gentle, so rightfully adoring, she cannot imagine
that there was ever a man who wished her dead at all.

For Keepsies with B

I call to tell you Mike got 3 years and he wants to know if you
can sell his weed for him. Hide the gun in his Skylark—*the cops
didn't find it, so he must've hid it somewhere good.* You sigh, say, *Shit.*
I say it back. We talk through the logistics of what to do
with a man's belongings while he's locked in a cage for 3 years,
and we're both scratching our heads. We briefly live in the joke
of you selling expired weed and maybe you'll just smoke
the whole stash instead.

When we were kids, you'd come stay the night and my mother
never made a big deal about the fact that you wet the bed
almost into middle school. Your whole room smelled like piss,
and even through all that stench, you dreamt of some place better
than this.

We'd race barefoot around the complex parking lot, alive
in the foggy dusk of a California summer, until we forgot
what it smelled like. We'd eat rootbeer barrels like kings
and use dimes to buy gum from Money Saver at the end
of the block. We'd stay up at night to argue over how long
cats stay pregnant and whether or not men can lactate. Dream
of veterinary school and homes of our own.
Childhood wasn't always heavy, and I owe you this memory.

We aren't just the kids who barely made it out
of the shit town our parents landed in.

At night you were drowning in your own piss while your parents
were getting loaded, but during the day we'd play marbles for keepsies
in the dirt until we forgot the stench. I love you. I love you more
than I've ever loved anyone.

I'll say it like this: You've got 2 dogs and a good love
now and your dad can't touch you and your mom's still
high, but you can't win it all. You've stopped selling weed
and you groom dogs during the day and clean up an
old folks home at night and I am so proud of you. It's been a long time
since circumstance has held you down and shoved your face
in piss and made you inhale.

In a different version of this story, we don't become shit.
In a different version, you couldn't dream through all that stench.
You couldn't cut through the smoke, but that alternate ending
isn't it. We're writing its eulogy, playing marbles on its grave.

Your Doctor Says Dementia

and of all the things that have not killed you,

how dare your memory be the one to do it?

Just like a woman—to die & leave her body behind. They've lifted

the lid off of you and found your memory is evaporating rain,

and I am lifting off with it. One day, maybe soon,

you won't remember the bunny cake you made

for my birthday—you'll wake up and you will not know that I was

your grand invention. One day you will walk the street and will not

remember the Rottweiler that bit in, so maybe you will reach out

to touch a beast. If they open you up (as they have), will memories

still be lost in the room of you? Hiding beneath a stack of bills

or at the bottom of your makeup bag?

Or is it rather—poof—gone now?

Every almost forgotten moment, a reason to move close to you.

But what would I do there? Have you recite your painful life

back to me? How much of you have you already forgotten

just to keep moving through the river of life? Wading and slipping

on smoothed rocks beneath. I cringe at the doctor's *resilient*. A word

to say you deserve to carry it all. I don't know whether to apologize or

thank biology for one day lifting all that trauma

from your bones.

At Last

In Kentucky in 2015, Kim Davis refuses to marry same-sex couples.

Kim; Let me tell you about my mother and her wife.
They found each other after 49 years. Their wedding was open
park in August. We all sat sweat drenched and rejoicing.

My mother walked the aisle to Etta James, At Last,
and at the sight of her my stepmother wept,
     and we should all want to love like that.
You think opinion can fit here?
     You think you are so mighty you can protest magic?
You and your stubborn bigot god shake your fist at love?

You must not know that love can heal an entire country,
make 2 women whole, pull them from the ashes of their own life.

You spend 5 days in jail and cry on camera.
     My mother spends 50 years in purgatory and loves, still.
You should learn to bow and pray to that glory, worship that God.

Kim, your moment will burn out and my mother, her wife, their 2
dogs will love, still,
                             At last.

Grief Vignettes for Kaiya

My friend Anna says we cannot write
someone's life into something as simple
as a poem. I say, I cannot write you into a poem
because you always have been one—you

lay in the dirt now. In a land
made entirely of your bone & sinew,
& up grows a new tree with your wild

blue hair—your new body.
Here, a new world blooms.

/ / /

I have so many memories of you,
how nostalgia has hardly touched them at all.
Just earlier it seems your hands offer up
a mango from your grandmother's tree

split in 2 we share.
& then blink. Gone.

/ / /

When you died, your mother on the other end of
the telephone line said she was holding your hand.
I wept in a cottage somewhere on the Australian
coast. Alone. For days, days.

/ / /

An unknown continent—this new world without you in it.

/ / /

I trudged into the Pacific barefoot and brought you with me—
though it was you that walked me
vast and blue.

There I tasted the salt on my lips
and it all ended
in laughter.

/ / /

I do not know which poem it will be that lays the grief
of you in the soil with your body.
This thought makes joy and misery neighbors in me.

/ / /

I do not say your name to summon someone
else's god. You are the God here. No religion or
myth paints you as brilliant as you always have
been. Your face does not belong to a god or casket
but belongs to our memory.

/ / /

Just yesterday I sat at your dinner table with your mother
and read your poems to her. Each word, you live. Each word,
a prayer. You—a God I can believe.

Of All the Muscles

in the human body
there is a reason why
the heart is the only one
we can hear.

A Series of Portraits More Intimate Than Sex

Beginning with a quiet hotel room and a love
who has just buried his father. Silent and unravelled
into the glow of HGTV. He asks only
for Dr Pepper and a burrito.

In the shower with tweezers
and he's pulling out a hair that grows from my nipple.

We're out at dinner and I accidentally fart
and he takes the blame.

He's slouched over sitting on the bed in his underwear
clipping my toenails.

Asleep next to each other at 2am
and our dog vomits raw meat onto our naked bodies.

We've just started dating and his apartment
is being fumigated. He finds my DivaCup in his medicine cabinet
and puts in a tupperware container.

It's 15 degrees and we're in a tent at the Grand Canyon
and he holds the water bottle so I can pee
and still stay under the covers.

Still the closest we've been has been on my birthday

when he gives me a new haircut—I lay
on the bed on my back and open my legs
and he gives my cunt a trim.

Lately, I've been falling asleep during our small rituals.
My whole body, limp under a razor blade in his hand.

You Became in a Town No One Has Ever Heard Of

Your father is dead and we are driving the long highway
to Chickasha, Oklahoma, and you tell me the proper way
to pronounce a town called Alex, said like Elick, and I don't argue.
The highway drags on and on, and as we round the handle
of your home state, shaped like a hatchet, you fall
quiet. Wrapped up inside the nostalgia that you were once a child
here and that invisible is still bottomless in you.
The fucked up truth is that this is where our love was born,
for better or worse, inside the hurt of our child selves,
and yes, your father is dead now, and mine is maybe
the same. Our kith and kin have been drowned in the dirt
and America is the taxidermist of our fathers.
The reason I love you like this is because I do
not have to explain this ache. It is now that I see
that I've spent all my life learning
the vocabulary of us. Our fathers were never ours,
but they were the hands of capitalism.
Once I thought my father wanted a daughter
but all he knew to want was an ax, and your father the oil.
We were not supposed to inherit the tenderness we give
each other. Your father has died, and it has opened a wound
in you that shows me a light. O, how I thank
the truck at 4am, the tree through your jaw,
and the straight edge that followed, the line that led you to me.
O, how I thank your father's fist and how you learned
who to be by what not to be: a fist. O, how I thank our mothers
for this capacity to love so full of mercy. How you wouldn't be the
man I love if it weren't for the crackpipe, the trailer park, the rehab,
the not-love your father knew and held fast, all the way to the grave.
O, Oklahoma and your grand and fucked up nothingness. O, sweet dirt
road and rounded bend that sat us into the silence of it all. O, how the
sharp edges of hurt have chiseled away at the gift of a life so pregnant
with possibility.

Ode to My Strap-On Dildo and Ode for My Love on His Hands and Knees in Front of Me

A man I love is bent before me & open
to what might be a bloody orgasm.
He braces for me, bowed & on all fours
the opposite of a prayer,
& in this ceremony I marry him
to the phantom limb we bought for 50 dollars
on the internet. We've grown close enough
to love this way & he is well enough to unclench
what can take a fist and I'll do that, too
but not now—I touch him in the way
those of us raised into girlhood know best.
Now I teach a man that has never opened to open
& so tenderness is the only safe passage here.
Gentle I pull into him. We have lived
our whole lives in a costume but in this room
we made for ourselves we have taken off the day
& we use a different muscle. I've purchased your cock,
oh manhood, & I offer it to my lover
and it is not a weapon but an invitation.
I've taken your precious phallus & used it
to reteach myself about intimacy.
This fake feeling-less appendage is the grandest teacher of consent.
I listen with the other parts of me. Ask every step of the way.
What can masculinity do to me now
that I've bought its trophy
and attached it to my body like a jetpack?
I'm soft & I know to go slow. I've learned
to never rush the unlearning. This is the sweetest
gift he's given me this morning & I will return
the generosity. He wants me to hallow him,
to let him feel what it is to hollow
himself around me, pull me in, & release.

All the Plus-Size Models in the Magazines Are Actually Regular Size

or While Having a Mild Panic Attack in the Bathroom Because I Have to Shop for Clothes in Front of Other People

1.

I look in the mirror and wonder how many bodies
look like mine in magazines.
Quite a few—all with the word *before* written underneath.

> (Now I need to tell you I have not always been this pre-transformation body. I have starved myself and I have been smaller than this and I feel that's important. I know what it is to hate myself enough to keep a tally of the parts of me that I have disappeared. To not have enough energy to take a shower and feel accomplished for it. I know what it's like to start a diet or a cleanse or starvation tactic and call it healthy. Coffee and a handful of blueberries and call it self care.)

I was 16 when my mother got weight-loss surgery

> (she was smaller than I am right now);

she looks at me and says she loves me.

> (She hates herself and loves me. We are the same.)

My love holds the body that I am in today,
and I hold back

> (a hate, a wish to be in another).

2.
On the best days, I hate
the world and love myself.

3.
Body: you are a good, good body.

Made of softness
of scars
of scabs
of fuck
fight
forget
come
undress
hide
come back like the moon.
Undo and hinge again
open
shrink.

Body, you are a bird with wings clipped.
Body, you are a quiet room.
Body, you are a home I made.
Every day I want to be an ode for you.
Let the days that my love for you is
rhizomatic and everywhere be most days.
I've called you a mistake but you are not one, never
have been, could not be on the worst day.

Body: you are a good, good body.

4.
Thank you, body, for being the only love
that is truly unconditional.

Some days I am so much more than a body,
and some days that's it, that's all.

Some days I cry while standing in front of the closet.
Some days I never look in a mirror.
Some days I do everything I can to be unseen.

But not everyday. But not today.
And I'll take that victory.

I Forgive You

My mother will tell you that I was a quiet child;
I will tell you I was born screaming and everyone looked away.

I once went 119 on the highway and no one stopped me.
I once dug my name into my thigh and no one bothered

to pronounce it. I once called my body sand, line drawn
with a razor—no one crossed it. That kind of invisible can make
a girl disappear into any mouth. I have spent
years dreaming of a girlhood with my lips not stitched

into a seam. Imagine: if my mother could say she loved me without
looking away, if my father knew my phone number,
if there was never a boy burying my face in the hardwood.

I would be anchored to resentment if I did not
let time take hold of memory. Witness me.

Look at the girl I was.
Look at the me I am.

                        Hear me say:

I forgive you, mother, for all the years you could not see me.
Searching for a quieter life, no children to hold
to your breast.

I forgive you, father. Even though you are a language
I do not speak.

I forgive you, boy who found me weeks after the ambulance did.

I forgive you, loves who did not love me back.

I forgive you, my love, for each night you thrash inside the darkness
of your head, drag yourself across the rocks of memory.

I forgive you, self, for all the years I could not love you.

That is the most resounding work song. To say: I forgive you.
I forgive you. And when I do not, I forgive myself for that, too.

When I wake with a past wrapped around my throat,
I forgive myself for that, too.

Take my filthy name. Let me call myself bird. Let me call myself
100 days of laughter. Call myself ice cream on the porch despite the
hot day. Call myself the sweet insides of a strawberry.
Let me call myself girl.

　　　Let me name myself for all the women I could have been.

Tighten my eyes, lay my body warm, flat in the dirt.
I plant my baby teeth like seeds and up grows a
girl who can lie in the sun where no man will touch her.

Each hole I dig, I whisper, I'm alive still,
and isn't that more than I was supposed to be?

Each hole I dig, I whisper, I forgive you.
I forgive you

I forgive you

I forgive you

I forgive you

I forgive you

I forgive you

I forgive you

I forgive you

I forgive you

I forgive you

I forgive you

I forgive you

I forgive you

I forgive you

I forgive you

I forgive you

I forgive you

I forgive you

I forgive you

I forgive you

I forgive you
I forgive you I forgive you I forgive you I forgive you I forgive you I
forgive you I forgive you I forgive you I forgive you I forgive you
I forgive you I forgive you I forgive you I forgive you I forgive you I

forgive you I forgive you I forgive you I forgive you I
forgive you I forgive you I forgive you I forgive you I forgive
you I forgive you I forgive you I forgive you I forgive you I forgive you I
forgive you I forgive you I forgive you I forgive you I forgive you I
forgive you I forgive you I forgive you I forgive you I forgive you I
forgive you I forgive you I forgive you I forgive you I forgive you I
forgive you I forgive you I forgive you I f o r g i v e y o u I forgive you
I forgive you I forgive you I forgive you I forgive you I forgive you I
forgive you I fo r g i v e you I forgive you I forgive you I forgive you
I forgive you I forgive you I forgive you I forgive you I forgive you I
forgive you I f o r g i v e y o u I forgive you I forgive you I
forgive you I forgive you I forgive you I forgive you I forgive you I
forgive you I forgive you I forgive you I forgive you I forgive you I
forgive you I forgive you I forgive you I forgive you I forgive you I
forgive you I forgive you I forgive you I forgive you I forgiveyouIforgive
youIforgiveyouIforgiveyouIforgiveyou I forgive you I forgive you I forgive
you I forgive you I forgive you I forgive you I forgive you I forgive
you I forgive you I forgive you I forgive you I forgive you I forgive
you I forgive you I forgive you I forgive you I forgive you I forgive
you I forgive you I forgive you I forgive you I forgive you I forgive
you I forgive you I forgive you I forgive you I forgive you I forgive
you I forgive you I forgive you I forgive you I forgive you I forgive
you I forgive you I   f   o   r   g   i   v   e
y   o   u   I forgive you I forgive you I forgive you I forgive you I
forgive you I forgive you I forgive you I forgive you I forgive you I
forgive you I forgive you I forgive you I forgive you I forgive you I
forgive you I forgive you I forgive you I forgive you I forgive you forgive
youIforgiveyouI forgive you I forgive you I forgive you I fo r g i v e you
I forgive you I forgive you I forgive you I forgive you I forgive you I
forgive you I forgive you

until it is true.

Book Notes

Previous versions of the following poems appeared in *The Year of the Institution*, Next Left Press, 2014: *One Side of an Ongoing Dialogue with Sharon, My Therapist, Señor Frogs*, and *I Break Like a Fever*.

Previous versions of the following poems appeared in *Dimly Lit*, Next Left Press, 2015: *Nine, The Gutter, The Funny Wind of the Heart Is Not a Reliable Weathervane*, and *B on Elm Street Behind the Fairgrounds, 1999*.

In "Knots," the phrase "speedtrap town" is borrowed from a Jason Isbell song.

"Sink" was inspired by Hieu Minh Nguyen's poem "Stubborn Inheritance."

In "You Became in a Town No One Has Ever Hear Of," the phrase "drowned in the dirt" is from the Jason Isbell song "Something More Than Free."

In "Pleasant Valley State Prison with Inmate Number F-49837," the phrase "invisible cloak of whiteness" is inspired by Sharon Olds' "Ode to My Whiteness."

"Where Did You Get That Pick-Up Line? You Should Drop It Back Off" was originally written in a text thread with my dear friend Sasha Banks.

Acknowledgments

This book of poems was only possible because my dogs, Kala and Leni, allowed me to sit at my desk for hours, while they looked on wishing I would hurry up and move to a more ideal spot in the house, one in which they could smother me.

Thank you to those who saw me when I was a young writer and believed I had a story to tell: Chancelier Skidmore, Donney Rose, Anna West, Sue Weinstein, Jocelyn Young, Geoff Munsterman, Chelsea Lynne Murry, Deandre Hill, Julia Roth, Joaquin Zihuatanejo, Giselle Robinson, Ava Haymond, Bill Moran, Kaycee Filson, Beck Cooper, Leslie Rose, the Baton Rouge poetry community, the New Orleans poetry community, and the slams across the country that heard many of the poems that brought me to these.

Thank you to those who saw these poems first: Christopher Diaz, Sierra DeMulder, Sasha Banks, Sam Gordon, and Anna Montague. I would not have had faith in myself if you did not show me how.

Thank you to those who dedicated hours to comb through this manuscript with me: Hieu Minh Nguyen, Olivia Gatwood, and Megan Burns. Thank you for your steady hands.

Gratitude to the institutions that granted me the space I needed: Forward Arts, The Eclectic Truth community, Slam New Orleans, Button Poetry, Word Bank, and The Heart of It.

Thank you, Brian Tetreault, for the lifelong love of a first true friend. We lived. We live.

My siblings, Michael, Laura, Christina, and Sophia, for allowing me the grace to tell our hardest truths. Without you there would have been no witness and no reason to tell a story at all. Thank you to my nieces and nephews for being a light when we needed to see a way out: Omar, Suhmarri, Key'Milleon, Gianna, Kanton, and Princeton.

My Button family. Thank you, Sam Cook, for believing in this project when it was only a seed, and thank you, Hanif Abdurraqib, for taking the book on and your unwavering faith in it. Dylan Garity, Neno Grae, and all of the hands hard at work giving those of us who aren't supposed to be given space all the space we need.

I am indebted to Alexis Sebilian, who is the greatest sisterfriend I could have imagined. You were the first audience for many of my poems, and I cannot repay you for every gentle push you gave me and the relief of re-capping each old episode of *Law & Order SVU* when the real world was just too much. Thank you, Grandmere, for being a grandmother, a friend, and a cheerleader I was gifted by Alexis.

And thank you to my mother, Vicki Heinrich—once you told me that sometimes you forget it ever happened at all. It did. It all did. And you, despite, walked me through the fire.

And to my deepest, truest heart, William Brian. How I would be lost deep in the hallways of myself without the freedom of your love. Thank you for pushing me, gently and with vigor, to my wildest dreams.

Desireé Dallagiacomo is a poet and educator originally from Chico, California. She is the program director for the youth spoken word organization, Forward Arts. She is a Pushcart Prize nominee and she has been a finalist at every major national poetry slam in the United States. She is the co-host of the Southern Poetry podcast, Drawl, and in 2016 she founded an annual writing retreat in rural New Mexico for emerging writers. Desireé lives in Baton Rouge, Louisiana with her partner, their cat, and their 2 rescue pitbulls. This is her first full-length collection of poems.

Other Books By Button Poetry

If you enjoyed this book, please consider checking out some of our others, below. Readers like you allow us to keep broadcasting and publishing. Thank you!

Neil Hilborn, *Our Numbered Days*

Hanif Willis-Abdurraqib, *The Crown Ain't Worth Much*

Olivia Gatwood, *New American Best Friend*

Donte Collins, *Autopsy*

Melissa Lozada-Oliva, *peluda*

Sabrina Benaim, *Depression & Other Magic Tricks*

William Evans, *Still Can't Do My Daughter's Hair*

Rudy Francisco, *Helium*

Guante, *A Love Song, A Death Rattle, A Battle Cry*

Rachel Wiley, *Nothing Is Okay*

Neil Hilborn, *The Future*

Phil Kaye, *Date & Time*

Andrea Gibson, *Lord of the Butterflies*

Blythe Baird, *If My Body Could Speak*

Available at buttonpoetry.com/shop and more!